821.08   First poems of
FIR   childhood
c.2

FIRST
POEMS
OF
CHILDHOOD

Illustrated by
TASHA TUDOR

Platt & Munk, Publishers/New York
A Division of Grosset & Dunlap

Pussy Willow   Kate Brown

Dairy Charm

The Hayloft   Robert Louis Stevenson

Who Has Seen the Wind   Christina G. Rossetti

The Slumber Boat   Alice C. D. Riley

The Months   Richard B. Sheridan

Baby   George MacDonald

The Table and the Chair   Edward Lear

Wings   A Psalm of David

Monday's Child

The Star   Jane Taylor

The Rock-a-by Lady   Eugene Field

At the Seaside   Robert Louis Stevenson

Pussy Willow

By KATE L. BROWN

Pussy Willow wakened
   From her winter nap,
For the frolic spring breeze
   On her door would tap.

"It is chilly weather
   Though the sun feels good.
I will wrap up warmly,
   Wear my furry hood."

Mistress Pussy Willow
   Opened wide her door.
Never had the sunshine
   Seemed so bright before.

Never had the brooklet
   Seemed so full of cheer:
"Good morning, Pussy Willow,
   Welcome to you, dear!"

Never guest was quainter:
   Pussy came to town
In a hood of silver gray
   And a coat of brown.

Happy little children
   Cried with laugh and shout,
"Spring is coming, coming,
   Pussy Willow's out."

Dairy Charm

Come, butter, come; come, butter, come.
  Peter stands at the gate
Waiting for his buttered cake;
  Come, butter, come.

Seventeenth Century

The Hayloft

By ROBERT LOUIS STEVENSON

Through all the pleasant meadow-side
  The grass grew shoulder-high,
Till the shining scythes went far and wide
  And cut it down to dry.

Those green and sweetly smelling crops
  They led in wagons home;
And they piled them here in mountain tops
  For mountaineers to roam.

Here is Mount Clear, Mount Rusty-Nail,
  Mount Eagle and Mount High;—
The mice that in these mountains dwell,
  No happier are than I!

Oh, what a joy to clamber there,
  Oh, what a place to play,
With the sweet, the dim, the dusty air,
  The happy hills of hay!

Who Has Seen The Wind?

By CHRISTINA G. ROSSETTI

Who has seen the wind?
    Neither I nor you:
But when the leaves hang trembling
    The wind is passing through.

Who has seen the wind?
    Neither you nor I:
But when the trees bow down their heads
    The wind is passing by.

The Slumber Boat

By ALICE C. D. RILEY

Baby's boat's the silver moon,
  Sailing in the sky,
Sailing o'er the sea of sleep,
  While the clouds float by.

Sail, baby, sail,
  Out upon that sea,
Only don't forget to sail,
  Back again to me.

Baby's fishing for a dream,
    Fishing near and far,
His line a silver moonbeam is,
    His bait a silver star.

    Sail, baby, sail,
        Out upon that sea,
    Only don't forget to sail,
        Back again to me.

The Months

BY RICHARD B. SHERIDAN

January snowy,
    February flowy,
        March blowy;

April showery,
    May flowery,
        June bowery,

July moppy,
      August croppy,
            September poppy;

October breezy,
      November wheezy,
            December freezy.

Baby

By GEORGE MacDONALD

Where did you come from, baby dear?
Out of the everywhere into the here.

Where did you get those eyes so blue?
Out of the sky as I came through.

What makes the light in them sparkle and spin?
Some of the starry spikes left in.

Where did you find that little tear?
I found it waiting when I got here.

What makes your forehead so smooth and high?
A soft hand stroked it as I went by.

What makes your cheek like a warm white rose?
I saw something better than anyone knows.

Whence that three-cornered smile of bliss?
Three angels gave me at once a kiss.

Where did you get this pearly ear?
God spoke, and it came out to hear.

Where did you get those arms and hands?
Love made itself into hooks and bands.

Feet, whence did you come, you darling things?
From the same box as the cherubs' wings.

How did they all just come to be you?
God thought about me, and so I grew.

But how did you come to us, you dear?
God thought about you, and so I am here.

The Table and the Chair

By EDWARD LEAR

Said the Table to the Chair,
"You can hardly be aware
How I suffer from the heat
And from chilblains on my feet.
If we took a little walk;
We might have a little talk;
Pray let us take the air,"
Said the Table to the Chair.

Said the Chair unto the Table,
"Now, you *know* we are not able:
How foolishly you talk,
When you know we *cannot* walk!"
Said the Table with a sigh,
"It can do no harm to try.
"I've as many legs as you:
Why can't we walk on two?"

So they both went slowly down,
And walked about the town
With a cheerful bumpy sound
As they toddled round and round;
And everybody cried,
As they hastened to their side,
"See! the Table and the Chair
Have come to take the air!"

But in going down an alley,
To a castle in a valley,
They completely lost their way,
And wandered all the day;
Till, to see them safely back,
They paid a Ducky-quack,
And a Beetle, and a Mouse
Who took them to their house.

Then they whispered to each other,
"O delightful little brother,
What a lovely walk we've taken!
Let us dine on beans and bacon."
So the Ducky and the leetle
Browny-Mousy and the Beetle
Dined, and danced upon their heads
Till they toddled to their beds.

Wings

Oh that I had wings like a dove!
For then would I fly away and be at rest.
Lo, then would I wander far off,
And remain in the wilderness.

A Psalm of David

Monday's Child

Monday's child is fair of face,
Tuesday's child is full of grace,
Wednesday's child is full of woe,
Thursday's child has far to go,
Friday's child is loving and giving,
Saturday's child works hard for its living,
And a child that's born on the Sabbath day
Is fair and wise and good and gay.

There is one little dream of a beautiful drum—
    "Rub-a-dub!" it goeth;
There is one little dream of a big sugarplum,
And lo! thick and fast the other dreams come
Of popguns that bang, and tin tops that hum
    And a trumpet that bloweth!

And dollies peep out of those wee little dreams
    With laughter and singing;
And boats go a-floating on silvery streams,
And the stars peek-a-boo with their own
        misty gleams,
And up, up, and up, where the Mother
        Moon beams,
The fairies go winging!

Would you dream all these dreams that are
        tiny and fleet?
    They'll come to you sleeping;
So shut the two eyes that are weary, my sweet,
For the Rock-a-by Lady from Hushaby Street,
With poppies that hang from her head to her feet,
    Comes stealing; comes creeping.

At the Seaside

By ROBERT LOUIS STEVENSON

When I was down beside the sea
A wooden spade they gave to me
To dig the sandy shore.
My holes were empty like a cup,
In every hole the sea came up,
Till it could come no more.